Practical Networking:
How to Give and Get Finding Jobs

Practical Networking:
How to Give and Get Finding Jobs

By
Edward L. Flippen

Practical Networking: *How to Give and Get Finding Jobs*
Copyright © 2023 by Edward L. Flippen

All rights reserved. No part of this book may be reproduced, restored in a retrieval system, or transmitted by means, electronic, mechanical, photocopying, recording, or otherwise, without written consent from the author.

ISBN:979-8-98751-2500 (Paperback)
ISBN:979-8-98751-2517 (Hardcover)
ISBN: 979-8-98751-2524 (eBook)

Contents

Introduction ... vii

Chapter 1
Jobs, Jobs Everywhere and Not A Job To Be Found ... 1

Chapter 2
Fired ... 2

Chapter 3
In-Law to the Rescue ... 3

Chapter 4
Networking ... 5

Chapter 5
Friends ... 7

Chapter 6
Special People ... 10

Chapter 7
Church Friends ... 12

Chapter 8
Helping Strangers ... 14

Chapter 9
Helping Your Children ... 16

Chapter 10
Silver Bullets ... 19

Chapter 11
Political Bullets ... 22

Chapter 12
Wasting Contacts ... 24

Chapter 13
Advocates ... 26

Chapter 14
Mentors ... 28

Chapter 15
Shoot High ... 31

Chapter 16
Bothersome People ... 33

Chapter 17
Cold Calling ... 35

Chapter 19
Job Politics ... 38

Chapter 20
   Résumé Help   40

Chapter 21
   Rehearsing   42

Chapter 22
   References   45

Chapter 23
   Want Ad Help   48

Chapter 24
   Down And Out   50

Chapter 25
   Get A Plan: Gut It Out   53

Chapter 26
   Little Things Count   56

Chapter 27
   Leaving Private-Sector Jobs   59

Chapter 28
   Leaving A Government Job   62

Chapter 29
   What Goes Around Comes Around   65

Chapter 30
   A True Friend   66

Conclusion   69

INTRODUCTION

My mother, who Is my grandmother although I call her mother because she raised me from the time I was only a few weeks old, never owned a car; she never learned to drive; and she never had a job except for keeping boarders. Yet, we were never hungry. We always had clean clothes and lived in decent neighborhoods.

My mother and I have survived because she worked hard and instilled in me at an early age the importance of having a good job and being a hard worker. I began earning my keep, so to speak, before age twelve by mowing our neighbors' lawns. At age twelve, I began carrying the local evening newspaper and later the morning paper. In high school, I was a "distributive education student." That meant I went to school for half a day and worked the other half. My high school jobs included working for an Army and Navy store, an A&P grocery store, a printing firm, and I sold magazines, and rewound film for a state government agency.

I served three years in airborne units in the Army following graduation from high school. After military service, I worked for a small loan company and a local stock brokerage firm (in clerical positions) while attending college—mostly taking morning and night classes. Later, I worked as a stockbroker in Washington and New York. After graduate school, I was a college instructor. After law school, I was a college professor, a government lawyer, a regulatory lawyer, and for the last thirty years I have practiced law with a major law firm and taught at nationally-ranked colleges and universities.

I have been unemployed and had to survive on unemployment checks. I know how it feels to earn $1.25 an hour ($.10 an hour above the minimum wage in 1962), but I also know how it feels to earn a million dollars in a year. I have never had any formal training in human resources or personnel management, but I have spent a lifetime looking for jobs and helping others find jobs. I know how important jobs are to a person's mental, emotional, and physical well-being.

This book is about my experiences in helping get jobs and helping others get jobs. It's about our most valuable resource—our friends— and how they can help with jobs and job promotions. I know. "I get by with a little help from my friends." (John Lennon, song lyrics, 1967, with Paul McCartney)

CHAPTER 1
JOBS, JOBS EVERYWHERE AND NOT A JOB TO BE FOUND

Jobs are plentiful. They have been for most of my life. They've been more plentiful during some periods than others, but the number of jobs available and your ability to find a job are not variables with which you should concern yourself. We often hear the phrase, "It's a good job market for MBAs, engineers, computer programmers," or whatever. So what! Whether it's a good or bad job market, it's usually difficult even under the best of circumstances for the person looking for a job, a good one.

The periodic announcements on the television and by state and federal agencies that jobs are increasing usually relate to the increase in want-ad advertising, high-school drop-out rates, the number of businesses calling on college recruiters, and the drop in the number of people applying for unemployment. Such data are aggregate data. It predicts the direction of the economy, but it tells you very little about how likely it is that you will find a job you want in your particular field.

Indeed, optimistic announcements about the availability of jobs can make you feel inadequate if you're not connecting with an employer. It really makes you feel inadequate when you can't even get an interview. And it happens to the best of us.

But please, don't be depressed about searching for a job. If the economy is slowing—even with only the smallest percentage increase in growth—there are plenty of job opportunities. Simply because you can't find one does not mean there are no jobs available or that you will not find a job. It simply means that you can't get yourself a good job through your connections or efforts. It doesn't mean that friends can't help you get a job. They can and most will. "... friendship is precious, not only in the shade, but in the sunshine of life; and thanks to a benevolent arrangement of things, the greater part of life is sunshine." (President Thomas Jefferson, letter to Maria Cosway, October 12, 1786)

CHAPTER 2

FIRED

In 1969, after working as a stockbroker with a Washington, D.C., brokerage firm for one year, I left my job to pursue a doctorate in business administration at the University of Virginia. My doctoral work, however, was short-lived. Soon after enrolling in that program, I met my wife-to-be and we were engaged. Unfortunately, my prospective in-laws' first impression of me was far from favorable. They were simply not accustomed to their daughter dating someone who was drawing an unemployment check. Thus, in late 1969, at age thirty, I hit the pavement in the "Big Apple" looking for a Wall Street job that, I thought, would impress them.

I quickly found a job. After only six months on the "street" as a stockbroker, however, I was told that my services were no longer needed. This was my first (and, I hope, only) experience receiving a "pink" slip. It was devastating news. My wife and I were newlyweds and, worse yet, she was six months pregnant. We had no money, no job, no car, and a baby on the way. I wondered, how could a Virginian like me get a job in New York City if he had only been there six months, didn't know anyone, and had been fired from the only job he'd had in the "Big Apple"? I quickly realized I couldn't. So I packed up and moved out.

We packed a U-Haul truck, and with me in the truck and my wife in the car we had borrowed from my father-in-law, we headed home to Virginia. Moving out of New York proved almost as challenging as keeping my job in New York. My wife went through one lane of the Holland Tunnel and I and my U-Haul down another. We lost each other for hours. I couldn't even find my way out of New York. How, I asked myself many times, was I ever going to find a permanent job? What I didn't realize was that "in the middle of difficulty lies opportunity." (Albert Einstein)

CHAPTER 3

IN-LAW TO THE RESCUE

With the exception of service during World War II, my father-in-law spent his entire career teaching law. He was an exceptional teacher, but he had no experience in finding a job for a fired stockbroker. He also wasn't the type of person who made claims of having great contacts. Nevertheless, his quiet assistance was invaluable to me, although I did not fully appreciate it at the time.

After being booted off the "Street," and after a stint living with my in-laws, I landed a college teaching job in Harrisonburg, Virginia. It was less pay than I had made as a stockbroker in New York, and considerably less pay than I had made as a stockbroker in Washington, D.C. Regardless, it was a dignified job. Moreover, my wife and I now could pay the rent.

But I didn't get the job because the college was recruiting former stockbrokers. No way. It was because my father-in-law, in his quiet and distinguished manner, had urged the college to consider me. There were certainly other qualified candidates, but they considered and ultimately hired me because they knew and respected his opinion. He was a man of the highest integrity and had an outstanding professional reputation; his recommendation was worth far more than any claims I could ever make about myself.

At the conclusion of the academic year, I decided to attend law school, so my wife and I left for law school with a new baby girl and our bills paid. Since that time, I have never refused to help anyone who has sought my assistance to find a job. In fact, I know I can often do a better job helping someone get a job than they can do for themselves; can do for myself. I have learned from years of experience that the best people to help you get a job are the people who know you and care about you—your family and friends. But for reasons beyond the scope of this book, and probably for reasons deeper than could be explained in a graduate psychology book, they're often the last people we approach for help with our job search. This is a big mistake. They are the people who want to help and, equally important, can do you the most good for a quite simple reason. They know you the best. Ask your in-laws for help. Ask your father, mother, brothers and sisters, uncles and aunts, cousins, and nieces and nephews. And don't forget your grandparents. You could be surprised about whom they know and who might be honored to assist them or their grandchild. People who care about you will be genuine in their assistance. "Never hesitate to hold out your hand; never hesitate to accept the outstretched hand of another." (Pope John XXIII)

CHAPTER 4
NETWORKING

"Networking," a term that emerged in the 1980s, suggests that contacts can produce good job opportunities. It appears that many authors of "networking" books believe that they have made a new discovery: people who "network" have better chances at good jobs than they would otherwise have. To quote the author of one such book, "networking is the lifeblood of the job search."

It is interesting that many view the idea that people can benefit from contacts as a new concept. People have been benefiting from the right contacts since Old Testament times. For example, chapters 40 to 42 of the book of Genesis present an account of how the Pharaoh of Egypt's chief baker, who had been in the same prison as Joseph, a Hebrew, touted Joseph to interpret the Pharaoh's dreams. Joseph's interpretation of the Pharaoh's dreams eventually led the Pharaoh to put Joseph in charge of all of Egypt. What then is new about "networking"? Beats me, except that people didn't call it "networking" until relatively recently.

Regardless of whether "networking" is the buzz word du jour, it is not contacts that get you job offers; it is not hobnobbing with politicians and powerful businessmen and businesswomen; it is not being a member of the country club; and it is not being a good golf partner. Of course, everything has an exception and any one such contact could produce a job offer. But I would not bet on it. Not in a New York minute.

Instead, "good" job offers result from being qualified for the particular job you are seeking. True, that has not always been the case. In the 1950s and 1960s, people like me with a general education at the high school or college level were often employed as trainees. We were entry- level employees who received "OJT" (on the job training). Whatever the profession, people were often able to enter a particular field with only a high school or college general education. All they needed was to have completed school and to know the right people.

But long gone are the days when the older "good old boys" help the younger "good old boys" get jobs without regard to specific qualifications. Today's job seekers must have the precise qualifications an employer is looking for. The major businesses in the United States have reinvented themselves to compete internationally. To compete globally means having the best workers on the globe, and we're not talking about just computer jobs, information technology specialists, architects, engineers, and chemists. We're also talking about draftsmen, welders, electricians, editors, librarians, secretaries, switchboard operators, and every other job you can name. The former Herb Kelleher, the chairman, president and CEO of Southwest Airlines, was asked in a story in the Wall Street Journal in the summer of 1999, "Have the requirements for being a successful corporate leader changed much in your 30-plus years here [at Southwest Airlines]?" Mr. Kelleher responded: "When I started out, it was knowing people. It was being connected, like to the New York financial community. Anyone who wants to be successful these days can't afford to hire by the old school tie. The world is too competitive."

What I have tried to do for the last thirty-plus years is to be an advocate for people who were qualified for the job they sought. "Networking" may help with an introduction, but it is not a substitute for qualifications—not by any stretch of the imagination—and certainly not in a globally-competitive environment that is only going to become increasingly competitive in the next millennium.

Friends can help you get a job, but only the job you're qualified to get. Don't fool yourself into thinking that by "networking" you can get a job that someone else is better qualified for. If that's your approach to job hunting, you will be as lost as Dorothy: "Toto … I have a feeling we're not in Kansas anymore."

CHAPTER 5

FRIENDS

Make no mistake about it, if you have the qualifications, a friend can do for you in the job market that which you can never do for yourself. He can strongly sell your good qualities without any embarrassment, and he won't be concerned about your negative qualities. If someone starts out recommending someone by saying "Joe is a good guy, but ..." it doesn't make any difference what the "but" is. He's not a genuine friend unless, of course, he has talked to you about the "but" first.

If you're looking for a job and not asking your friends to help, you're not using some of your most valuable resources. Yes, I know. You don't want to bother your friends. Well, I respectfully disagree. Friends want to be bothered. Besides, they aren't really bothered when they're asked for help by a friend. The highest tribute you can pay to a friend is to let him or her know you need and want his or her help. You may not be able to help yourself. But I guarantee you that your friends can help you; and I guarantee you that they want to help. That's why they're friends. They see your best qualities. Quality products sell; anyone can sell quality and your friends can sell you.

Years ago, a banker friend of mine was in a high-level position at a Tennessee bank. He had a great job, but he was unhappy with his particular location. His unhappiness had nothing to do with the quality of life in Tennessee; he simply wanted to relocate to his native Virginia. He telephoned to tell me of his desire to secure a job in Richmond. At the time, I had a wonderful job in Charlotte, North Carolina; I was not really able to do much legwork to help him locate a job in Richmond. Nevertheless, I called a friend in Richmond who also was a banker. Because I had known my Tennessee banker friend for years, I could talk about his good qualities without preparation and from the heart. I knew nothing about banking, but I knew lots about my Tennessee banker friend, and all the things I knew about him were good things.

My banker friend in Richmond made a determined effort to find a job for my Tennessee banker friend and he was successful. My Tennessee banker friend now has retired from his Richmond job— and he retired doing quite well. His employment in Richmond was directly attributable to my Richmond friend's willingness to help me help another friend. My Richmond friend's willingness to help was directly attributable to our friendship. This is probably the best example of friends helping friends get a job. It also illustrates how a friend like me, who has no knowledge about a friend's job, can help anyway.

By happenstance, another friend had held a high-level federal government job in Tennessee several years earlier. That friend was not looking for a job, but when I heard of a top-level state government job in his field in Virginia, I called and asked if he would be interested. He expressed great interest but doubted whether I could help him. I had an entry-level government job; I certainly had no influence with high-level government executives. But what I did have in my job was a mentor in state government who trusted my judgment. I told my mentor of my friend and his considerable credentials. I added that he was an individual of the highest integrity, and that absolutely no one would ever regret hiring him. My mentor agreed to meet my friend, and after that meeting, agreed that he was the best possible candidate for the job. He then made a considerable effort to get his bosses to hire my friend. My mentor was successful, and my friend enjoyed a remarkably successful government career. More important, everyone who's ever known or worked with him agrees that he was the best possible person for this high-level government job. He has made us all proud.

The last story has an odd twist. It concerns how a friend helped a friend who wasn't even looking for a job to get a job. But it's not unusual for friends to look out for each other in all walks of life, so when you know of a job that is a "perfect fit" for a friend, seek it for your friend. Friends will not be offended that you are looking for opportunities for them, regardless of whether they're looking to change jobs at that point in their career.

I accepted a job with a law firm in Richmond in 1980 without knowing the requisites for success in the job. For example, I did not understand the need for client or business development. I thought that all lawyers did was "practice" law, without realizing that you can't practice law (or practice anything) without clients. Fortunately, a friend in law practice in Richmond knew how important it was for me to have my own clients. So, he started recommending me to businesses before I had even arrived on the job. I created a favorable first impression with my new employer when I walked through the door with clients. In fact, my friend's efforts "jump started" my legal career. I truly doubt if I could have gotten started by myself. But with my friend's help, I got started quite well and was able to maintain the momentum for the next fifteen-plus years. This is a terrific example of a friend anticipating another friend's needs in a new job and helping him in advance. It's the crème de la crème of friends helping friends.

Admittedly, sometimes helping friends secure a really good job is just plain luck. In 1974, I was teaching at Ohio State University. In a conversation with another faculty member in the faculty lunchroom, I happened to mention that I had a friend in Virginia who taught at a state university. The Ohio State faculty member and my friend were in the same field. Although I had no knowledge of their field, I did have considerable knowledge of the personal qualities of my friend. Also, I knew that he was an outstanding teacher. After hearing me describe my friend and his background, the Ohio State faculty member became interested in my friend and suggested that I have him send his résumé for consideration as a visiting professor. I followed up on the opportunity and the rest is history. My friend taught at Ohio State for a year, and during that year developed a professional relationship with members of his department. They collaborated on an advanced textbook that is now in its third printing. My friend has reached the top of his profession in teaching and research, and I have considerable pride that I was able to play a small part in opening the door to his brilliant career.

But, for sure, I am not always successful in helping friends. I recall when the daughter of a friend was nearing graduation from college. She was an exceptionally talented young woman who wanted to teach in a specialized field in science. Although she had a science background, she did not have her teaching credentials. I offered to help her find a suitable teaching job, but it was difficult. I had no background in her subject area, and it was virtually impossible for me to describe her specialty to friends and acquaintances, much less to strangers. Regardless, I wrote a number of letters recommending her based on my knowledge of her, her family and their personal qualities. I was not successful in getting her a suitable job. The closest we came was an opportunity for a temporary teaching job. She, however, could not accept that job because it started before her graduation. Eventually, she took a job in another field. I was sad that I couldn't help her, but she always appreciated how hard I tried. We can't always be successful, but we can always try. "You may be disappointed if you fail, but you are doomed if you don't try." (Beverly Sills).

CHAPTER 6

SPECIAL PEOPLE

We all have special people in our lives, people who are high school or college friends, sorority sisters or fraternity brothers, former GI buddies, mentors, fellow golfers, tennis partners, fellow church members, family, traveling companions, jogging partners, bowling partners, the lunchroom club, a former high school teacher, or others. Our special friends are people we can talk to in confidence. We give each other advice; we are there for each other.

Of course, not all special friends can get you a job. Many people do not have job contacts and many who have job contacts simply don't feel comfortable assisting others with jobs. Regardless, special friends will help as best they can and, often, if they can't personally help you, they will put you in contact with someone who can.

I have been blessed with several special friends who have helped me get business or helped others find jobs. In one instance, after several unsuccessful attempts to help a good friend's daughter find a job, I called a special friend and pleaded for his help. Reluctantly, he hired her himself. She stayed several years and did a great job. In another instance, the same special friend hired a good client's daughter after I was unsuccessful in helping her find a good job. She also turned out to be a gem of an employee. Indeed, my friend has never regretted hiring either person. In other instances, he has introduced people he didn't know to other employers simply because I asked for his help. He will do anything he can to help me help others. He's one of those "special people" in my life. Obviously, there are only a few people you can turn to who can hire someone. But there are those "special people" who, while unable to hire everyone you present to them, are willing to help you by finding someone else who can help.

I once spent a couple of years trying to help a friend's son get a job. He had lots of qualifications, but no experience. Most of his adult life had been spent pursuing college degrees in different fields. The result was that by the time he was nearly thirty, he had two undergraduate degrees and one graduate degree, but no field and no experience. He was desperate.

His mother and father, who are close personal friends, also were desperate, and I became desperate, too.

At first, I thought it was impossible to help my friend's son. It was obvious when he discussed his future that he had no interest in any specific field. It also was clear to me that his lack of direction came through in interviews. In any event, I have a special friend who works for a quasi-governmental agency who will do anything she can to help her friends. I called and pleaded with her to help my friend's son. She didn't make any promises but went to great lengths to help. She checked every job posting in her agency and put in a good word with department heads as jobs became available. Eventually she found something that was a "fit" (or at least a "loose fit") for my friend's son. He took the job and stayed for several years before changing jobs. I don't doubt for a second that his experience in the quasi-governmental agency helped qualify him for his next job. All he needed was help in getting his first job.

Calling upon special people for help should be your highest priority in your job search. Special people are so because they help their friends, no matter what the circumstances. If you're reluctant to ask special people for help, you are not utilizing available resources; you are diminishing your chances of finding good job opportunities; you're not being smart and you will be sorry. Each of us has a special friend in our life. "Relations are made by fate, friends by choice." (French poet Abbé Jacques Delille)

CHAPTER 7
CHURCH FRIENDS

Don't skip this section simply because you don't attend church. You probably know church people and/or know people who know church people. Whatever your religious beliefs, don't discount the willingness of church friends to help others, particularly their church friends. Often, church friends will go the extra mile because of that relationship.

My wife and I have known a particular family in Richmond for more than thirty years, and I knew the family before we were married. They are wonderful people, and we love them dearly. Some years ago, the father of the family passed away. Since then, we have tried to help whenever possible. When one of the children asked for our help in getting a job, we did our best. We helped with résumés, telephone calls, and most importantly, made ourselves available to discuss specific jobs and job strategies with them. I recall one instance when one of the children indicated an interest in an accounting-related job with a major retail company. We offered to help, particularly as one of the senior officers in the company and his wife were members of our church. Initially, our young friend applied for a job without success. My wife and I were especially disappointed because my wife had written a recommendation and directed it to this senior officer, and he had not responded. But my wife did not give up.

Soon thereafter, there was another vacancy at the same business. This time my wife wrote a "Dear" note on a copy of the earlier letter stating that she was disappointed that her young friend had not been contacted in my wife's earlier efforts to help her with a job. In fact, my wife pointed out that no one had even bothered to let her know the results of her young friend's job inquiry. My wife stated that she was writing a note on the original letter because she wasn't certain that the senior official had received the original letter.

Well, to make a long story short, our friend got a job on her second try and the senior official's secretary followed up to make certain there were no glitches the second time around. Suffice it to say, we appreciated the personal attention from the high-level official, but frankly, we expected such attention. My wife would not write a letter of recommendation to anyone about another person that was not accurate, and certainly not someone in our church she knows and respects. And while the first recommendation might have been ignored by a secretary, no able secretary would ignore a second letter from a church friend, particularly a letter expressing disappointment about not being contacted as a result of writing the first letter.

We never did know whether the senior official read my wife's first letter. It might have been that someone simply ignored it but, regardless, we doubted seriously that a second letter from a church friend would be ignored. As Shakespeare said, "All's well that ends well." Our young friend is still employed with the company and doing quite well.

I believe church friends are great contacts. They are relationships that simply cannot be replicated with other acquaintances. Church friends will help friends and friends of church friends; and even if they can't help directly because of a lack of personal involvement with particular companies and job opportunities, they can still help by telling others about your needs. Whatever they have to say about you will be considered from the heart; that's genuineness you can't buy. There is another and even more important reason to contact church friends or friends who have church friends. They not only will give you "help from the heart," they will pray for you. Looking for a job is difficult; friends can help with the difficulties you encounter; prayer can be the ultimate help. All things are possible through prayer. "When you affirm big, believe big and pray big, big things happen." (Norman Vincent Peale)

CHAPTER 8

HELPING STRANGERS

My secretary and I have helped, or at least tried to help, more than ninety people get jobs. They include secretaries, accountants, government employees, lawyers, new MBAs, financial analysts, bankers, judges, a physicist, school teachers, a facilities manager, paralegals, salespersons, and others. We don't discriminate. If you need help, and we can help, we will. Have typewriter—will type; have telephone—will talk; have feet—will walk.

Of course, it goes without saying that it is easier to help those you know. I have written letters and introduced people I don't know. But they're more difficult to help because it's hard to discuss a person you're not familiar with. Regardless, I still try to help people I don't know if they've been referred by someone I do know and care about. And sometimes I am able to help such people find appropriate jobs.

Several years ago, a friend in the federal government telephoned to ask if I could assist a young woman she had just interviewed for a job. My friend could not hire this woman, but she was quite impressed with her educational background and experience. She had an undergraduate degree from a highly regarded school and earned a 4.0 grade point average in an MBA program while working nearly full-time. The young woman was articulate and had considerable poise. At my friend's request, I met the young applicant. After a half-hour discussing her background, I wrote a letter of recommendation to an insurance company where I had a contact because she had expressed interest in the insurance field. The only question I had about her job prospects was whether the company would hire her before my letter reached the personnel office. I had no doubt that she would be able to find a job, and probably one that she wanted. All I had to offer was an introduction to an insurance company vice president. At best, I may have helped the young woman cut through the employment "red tape." But that's not really the point. I was there as backup if things didn't work out. Yes, people with perfect qualifications want help, even if it's from strangers.

There have been many other instances when my wife and/or secretary and I have tried to help strangers get jobs, but, again, it is a difficult task. In fact, when you contact friends about a stranger, their efforts are often a function of their relationship with you. But that doesn't mean you shouldn't ask friends to help you help people you don't know. Sometimes your friends can help in small but important ways, such as telling you whom to contact and telling you something about the contact person and/or about a particular position.

As a practical matter, in seeking help with your job search from a stranger, you must endeavor to meet with that stranger. A recommendation from the stranger is not likely to produce favorable results if the stranger must "make up" a recommendation. The best recommendation is one that is 100 percent genuine. For a stranger to be 100 percent genuine, he or she has to make a recommendation based on his or her knowledge about you. Therefore, at a minimum, you should meet the person you are asking to help so they can recommend you based on their impressions. In addition, you should provide them with a sample of your written work, if possible, so that they can judge your writing. Tell them about your background, discuss hobbies in which you have mutual interests so they can be enthusiastic about your interests; and keep them informed of your other job search efforts. It is difficult to help someone you don't know well find a job, particularly when they don't tell you whom they're talking to and the jobs that they're interviewing for. Also, keeping them informed about your job activities may trigger ideas and names of others they can call for help.

In short, don't turn down an offer from a stranger to help with a job search, but help him or her know something about you that he/she can be enthusiastic about. There is no substitute for a recommendation from an advocate. A friend of mine often says, "I'd rather have one advocate helping me than a hundred supporters." He's absolutely correct. But for someone to be your advocate, they've got to know you and like you; they've got to be enthusiastic about your future; they've got to believe in you. "If you'll believe in … [them], [they'll] believe in you." (Lewis Carroll)

CHAPTER 9

HELPING YOUR CHILDREN

Notwithstanding my experience in helping people get jobs, neither of my two daughters sought my help when they finished school and began their job searches. That children don't ask for help from their parents is not news. But parents find ways to help their children; I am no exception.

My first daughter was graduated from college in 1992 with a degree in interior design. She did quite well in school; she was enthusiastic about entering the job market; and she was focused on her career. She set out in the summer of 1992 to find a job, and within days she found an entry-level position in an interior decorator's store. Unfortunately, she did not realize that the job was principally a sales job. Yes, she was helping people decorate their homes and offices, but when all was said and done, it was really a retail sales job, and she was compensated on the basis of her sales. Interior decorating, she loved; retail sales she hated. My wife and I were stuck in the same house with a very unhappy child. It was no fun for her, and it was no fun for us.

After six months, my daughter was able to quit her retail job and, in effect, start over with the help of my hair stylist. I had explained my daughter's dilemma to my stylist (who is a woman). As we talked one day, I was thinking out loud about how great it would be for a major financial institution to hire my daughter as an intern to see if she would fit in. Generally, interior decorating services are outsourced, but there are a few interior designers in facilities management departments in financial institutions. I knew that as an intern, my daughter would be paid only minimum wage, but she would at least have the opportunity to demonstrate her enthusiasm, skills, industry and compatibility with other employees.

Well, as often happens when friends help each other, my hair stylist mentioned my intern idea to a high-level banking executive who thought it was a good idea. He told my stylist to have my daughter send in her résumé. She did and in a matter of days she was hired as an intern. The internship turned into a full-time job which afforded her considerable experience and the opportunity to meet and work with some of the finest people she has known.

My daughter stayed in her financial institution job for three years before joining an interior design firm. She genuinely appreciated the experience she gained from her former job and certainly appreciated the fact that without it, she would not have been able to break into her field. Indeed, her experience was so favorable, and the bank liked her so much it later hired her as an officer. It is amazing how a minimum-wage internship idea, passed on by my stylist, advanced my daughter's career. It is truly amazing. You can imagine why my stylist is now one of my best friends.

The story does not end with my first daughter. My second daughter was graduated from college four years later with a degree in English. She had no job prospects and, again, Dad was not consulted about getting a job. As I had done thirty years before, my younger daughter went to look for a job in the "Big Apple." Unfortunately, with no experience it was virtually impossible for her to get a job in New York City. Eventually, after many trips, filling out literally dozens of applications, and sending hundreds of résumés, she returned home to search locally.

By now you have guessed where I am heading. Yes, after my daughter returned, I went to my stylist and told her of my daughter's plight. How was I to find a job in the business world for a twenty-two-year-old English major who had no experience? Indeed, the only business experience she had was selling shoes at the local mall during her last two years of college. She was good at selling shoes, but she did not envision a career path as a shoe saleswoman. Nevertheless, my stylist mentioned my younger daughter to the same banker gentleman who helped my first daughter. He thought about it a while and then called my stylist and told her that the local banks were in the process of setting up banking operations in retail establishments such as grocery stores and Wal-Mart. With her background in retail, he believed that she would be a qualified candidate for such a job.

Lightning does strike the same place twice. My daughter applied for a job with his bank and was hired for a position in a retail establishment. She did quite well. In fact, so well that a year later she was hired away by a competitive bank and shortly thereafter was promoted to assistant manager and, less than a year later, to manager.

My younger daughter owes a lot to my stylist and her banker friend. My older daughter's husband works for the same bank. His recommendation was of considerable help. His enthusiasm for her, together with help from my stylist's banking friend, helped get her in the door. It took my stylist, her friend the banker, and my daughter's sister's husband; but that's how these things happen. It takes friends and family helping friends and family.

My situation is not unusual. Most children will listen to others more quickly than they will listen to their parents. The best way we can be a friend to a young person is to offer to advise them, particularly the children of our friends. My daughters think our friends are articulate, intelligent, rich, and "cool." Dad, of course, is none of the above. But that's okay. "Children aren't happy with nothing to ignore, and that's what parents are created for." (Ogden Nash)

CHAPTER 10

SILVER BULLETS

The Lone Ranger uses silver bullets because he wants to be certain that he doesn't miss. Not all of us have a six-shooter with silver bullets, but most of us have one friend, or a friend who has a friend, whom we can call on at least once for help when that particular friend is in a position to help. Simply put, a silver bullet is a unique opportunity that we have with a friend, acquaintance, or business relationship that may be a "single-shot" opportunity. Sometimes it's just the circumstances of the moment. For example, a business relationship that is not expected to last may be your silver bullet. During the period of that relationship, there could be a window of opportunity to help a friend get a job.

A silver bullet could be a father or mother who is in a unique position to help; it could be an aunt or uncle; it could be a former teacher; it could be a high-school friend or a college roommate; it could be an Army buddy, a fellow church member, a neighbor, a former Sunday school teacher, your first boss, the parents of your best friend growing up, your coworkers from your first job, your father's former boss, your mother's best friend, and so on. Somewhere out there is someone who will do whatever he can to make things happen for you and he is in a unique position to do it. He might not realize it; you might not realize it; but he's out there for you.

I have had a silver bullet or two in my life. In one instance, a close friend whom I helped get a job years ago helped me by hiring the daughter of my best client. He was in a unique position to hire someone, and he hired her because it was important to me. Several years later, the daughter of another close friend was in need of a job and, again, he came through for me. In both instances, I was desperate to help these young people get jobs. Their parents were special people who would do anything in the world for my family. My friend sensed my desperation. He would do anything to help me. He happened to be in a position to help, and so he did.

My friend has come back to me for professional help. I've always been there for him; I always will be. When I was desperate, he helped me; when he is desperate, I help him. We have been each other's silver bullet. I may have used up all my silver bullets with those two. He's not in the position to hire that he once was. Regardless, there is someone out there for you who is in a unique position.

Sometimes, of course, we can't help. We don't have the right contacts. But often we fail to recognize that what we can't do, our brother, sister, or spouse can. My wife has had a silver bullet or two. In one instance, she knew the president of a university because her father had worked with him for years. When a neighbor and friend was desperate to get a recommendation for her son to attend the university, my wife was able to help by writing the president directly. She had never done it before and has not done it since. But I felt she could make a difference; I believe she did. She knew both our friend's son and the president very well. She had the credibility with the president to write a personal and meaningful letter of recommendation. In another instance, which is discussed in chapter 6, she wrote the president of a major company on behalf of a daughter of a good friend.

My wife is a pre-school teacher. She doesn't have secretaries or a computer to help her crank out letters, and so when she does write, it's in longhand and that means a lot to the person she is writing. It's a special effort on her part and that detail and personal touch are not lost on the people reading her letters. She says she has no silver bullets left, but I suspect she has another one or two left and so I keep asking her for ways she can help and she keeps looking.

The long and short of it is that everyone, either directly or indirectly, probably has a silver bullet, i.e., a person who will help you and is in a unique position to get something done.

Unfortunately, we are often reluctant to ask for special help, particularly from people close to us, such as our parents, spouse, best friends, fellow church members, or others. We seem to think we should turn first to professional résumé preparers or placement services. Of course, it's easy to rationalize that your best friend, parent, uncle, and so forth would be helping if he or she could.

Because they're not, there's probably nothing they can do. That's often our attitude. But that is wrong. More often than not, they don't think or are unaware of how they can help, whom they should contact, what they should say. They also sometimes don't think about helping without being asked. Indeed, more often than not, they think that you have everything under control.

I have friends and acquaintances that I have asked to help me on behalf of someone I knew or someone I knew through someone else. Often the response was that they didn't want to use up their capital with respect to a particular employer because someone else they know better may need their help. However, the problem with saving your capital for the "right person" or "right circumstance" is that there may never be a "right person" or "right circumstance." If you have an opportunity to help someone—help them. You may never have as good an opportunity again. Time marches on. It would be a shame to have had opportunities to help others and pass up those opportunities for better opportunities to help which never come along. To quote Ben Franklin, "No morning sun lasts a whole day."

I have an acquaintance who says that "you should never do today what you can do tomorrow." I hope he's only kidding—at least when it comes to helping others. There may not be a tomorrow. If I am asked by a friend for help, I will help regardless of how much "capital" I use up. My concern is not that I will use up what goodwill I might have; my concern is that unique opportunities that I have to help others will pass me by and I won't have helped.

The daughter of a friend of my wife's completed an education program in a foreign country. She had no contacts in the business community in that country, and she was without the financial ability to job hunt there. At the time she contacted me for help, I was working on a major case for an important client of my law firm. The client very much appreciated my efforts on his behalf. I took advantage of our good relationship to ask his help for the young woman. My client's firm had significant overseas contacts, and I knew he could arrange interviews for her if he made the effort which, of course, depended on his attitude toward me. Simply put, I had a window of opportunity to help the young woman because of the good relationship I had with the client at that particular time. I took advantage of the opportunity; his contacts opened doors for her, and she found employment with an international firm. I knew I had a silver bullet with him (at least for that short while); I used it; and I'm glad I did. I might not have had it a week or a month later or ever again with this particular person.

I remember the Reverend Billy Graham being asked what he thought God would say to him on the judgment day. Reverend Graham said that he thought God would say that he didn't do enough. Well, if Billy Graham is concerned that he didn't do enough, I can't imagine how far behind I am in helping others. Maybe 10,000 years, I don't know. But I do know that I don't have time to pick and choose my spots to help others. If you have a unique opportunity to be a silver bullet for a friend, or a friend of a friend, or even the friend of a friend of a friend, use the opportunity today. We're all aging; our professional relationships change daily; we may not have today's opportunity tomorrow. "You cannot do a kindness too soon, for you never know how soon it will be too late." (Ralph Waldo Emerson)

CHAPTER 11

POLITICAL BULLETS

Silver bullets are lasting bullets. Why else would the Lone Ranger use them? Political bullets are short-lived. Nevertheless, they can be just as effective as silver bullets.

Most of us don't think of ourselves as "political" and we don't consider that we have "capital" with politicians. But, in fact, many of us have some form of "political capital," either directly or indirectly. Many of us have stuffed envelopes for politicians, handed out leaflets, attended fund-raisers, made political contributions, attended rallies, or spoken in favor of candidates to neighbors, fellow employees, and friends. And for those of us who don't do any of the above, we know people who are involved in politics or we know people who know people who are involved in politics. Thus, without realizing it, many of us have at least an indirect "pipeline" to politicians.

In my experience, politicians are genuinely grateful for the support they receive from their constituents, regardless of the nature of the support. That gratitude, however, is often short-lived because most politicians begin planning their next campaign as soon as they complete their last one. That's the nature of the beast. The long and short of it is that grateful politicians may not be as grateful tomorrow as they are today. Thus, there is a window of opportunity to get assistance from grateful politicians for jobs (or any other type of assistance), but the window will close sooner rather than later.

I have asked politicians for help in locating jobs for myself and for others. I can't claim unlimited success, but I have had some successes, particularly in getting help for others. For example, a well-known politician in my area came to my house one year for a Christmas party. At the end of the evening, I expressed my appreciation for his attendance, and he expressed his appreciation for my loyal support. Following the Christmas party, I wrote and asked for his help in securing a position for a recent law school graduate who had a particular expertise in a high-tech field. My letter was sent to a congressional committee by my political friend's office. I don't believe for a second that I got the young man a job, but I do believe that I helped get his foot in the door. After that, he got the job on his own. The point, however, is that I knew that my best opportunity to garner support for the young man was at the time that I was most appreciated by my political friend. (I might add that I did not feel that I was taking advantage of my political friend. I believe that the young man I was recommending was an exceptionally qualified young man.)

In a similar circumstance a few years later, I assisted a young woman in obtaining a high-level government appointment by writing a letter of support for her immediately following the successful election of the candidate for whom she wanted to work. The candidate was most appreciative of the work done by all of his supporters and, indeed, took the unusual step of calling many of them and personally thanking them. His appreciation of my support meant to me that he would at least consider any recommendation that I sent him about a prospective employee to serve in his new administration. Thus, I sent a strong letter of recommendation about a truly talented young woman of integrity. While she was certainly competing with other people equally talented, I believe my recommendation was timely and, again, got her foot in the door when others might not have been so lucky. Once in the door, she, of course, excelled on her own.

There have been other instances when there was a window of opportunity to get support from successful politicians and I have taken advantage of that to help find jobs for people that I believed were qualified. There are, of course, many instances when the opportunity was short-lived. Indeed, there are more instances of the latter than the former. But I am never discouraged. When I failed, I usually assumed that my timing was just poor. I never assumed that I should quit trying to get help from politicians in finding jobs for others. Their job is to help their constituents.

A final point on "political bullets." I never consider that asking others, including politicians, for help in locating jobs for qualified people is an imposition. I recommend people because I genuinely believe that they are good people who will do a good job. Sure, some individuals are not the best qualified candidate for a particular job and, consequently, they don't get that particular job. That happens. Regardless, everybody has good qualities; it's just a matter of trying to match their qualities with the right job. But when you have a friend with the right qualities for a particular job, and you know a politician who could potentially help that person get the job, you have a "political bullet." When you have a political bullet, shoot it—and shoot it fast. "A week is a long time in politics." (Harold Wilson, Prime Minister, 1964-70; 1974-76)

CHAPTER 12

WASTING CONTACTS

There is one lesson that I have learned about how *not* to help others find jobs. It is a lesson I learned the hard way and will never forget: *do not waste your contacts.* Don't casually mention a friend in the hopes that something positive may develop. I call that the "jobs by luck" approach. I know many people who claim to have obtained their "jobs by luck." Personally, I doubt it. "In the long run, men only hit what they aim at." (Henry David Thoreau)

In the mid-1980s, I had a client who became a good friend. We worked closely together on highly technical issues related to the communications industry. In the early 1990s, he was a senior vice president with a major communications company in the Midwest. As a result of his company's downsizing, he was "downsized"—but in style. He received a significant bonus and his salary for a year after he left the company. He moved to Richmond and he and I started having casual conversations about job opportunities in Virginia. Thinking that things would work out because of his strong technical and management background in both industry and government, I started sending him around town to meet business and government leaders. After the first year or so of "casual contacts," he began to take his job search more seriously. Now, he was off the payroll. So together we began a job search for him "in earnest."

What happened after that was something I did not anticipate. The people that I was sending him to see "in earnest" were mostly the same people I had sent him to see "casually." The reactions were such as "Ed, is [your friend] serious about a job?" or "Ed, what does he really want to do?" In short, I suddenly realized that I had "tainted" him by sending him to make "casual contacts" without a particular job objective.

For the next year (the third year after his departure from his Midwest job), he and I got quite serious about getting him a job. But it was tough sledding; I had used up my contacts. I felt more desperate than he did; after all, I was the one who had "tainted" him. I am convinced he would have done better had I not tried to be helpful (in my casual approach).

Finally, after reading the want ads in numerous newspapers for months, I found an ad for a job that was a perfect fit. I faxed it to him; he got an interview and was hired immediately. He still has the position and now helps me with others. He is a brilliant individual with exceptionally good qualifications. He would have done well without my assistance; in fact, better without my assistance.

My experience in helping this particular friend is one that I will never forget. Now, whenever I hear someone say: "I'm going to send out a résumé to see what happens"; or "how about mentioning my name"; or "I think I will stop by and let so and so know I am in the market"; I usually respond: "please don't" or "no, no, no." Job searching is one of the most serious things that we do in life. It should be taken just as seriously as decisions about marriage and having children. Whatever else you do, don't let yourself be viewed as someone who isn't serious about a job. "Everything must be taken seriously, nothing tragically." (Louis Adolph Thiers, French statesman and historian)

CHAPTER 13
ADVOCATES

There are a lot of different approaches to job hunting. But when all is said and done, there is one particular approach that is typically more fruitful than any other. It's not having a hundred friends (although that should help); it's not writing 500 letters (although that won't hurt); and it's not having a résumé prepared by a professional (although that could make your résumé impressive). It is having your own advocate.

Remember my friend who says that he would rather have "one advocate than a hundred supporters"? Over the years, I have come to realize the value of his statement (although he never said it in the context of getting a job). My friend is a lobbyist. He seeks approval of legislation on behalf of his clients. He would rather have one legislator committed to his legislation than a dozen simply giving their nodding approval. "One person with a belief is a social power equal to 99 who have only interests." (John Stuart Mill) This advice is valuable and transferable. It applies equally to job hunting.

If you have a lot of people cheering for you—patting you on the back, so to speak—that's great. We all need cheerleaders. But what is most helpful in a job search is having an advocate, someone who will advocate for you just as a lawyer does for a client, or as a teacher does for a child, or as a coach does for his athletes.

Advocates can do for you what you cannot do for yourself. Advocates see your best qualities; advocates speak and write about your best qualities; advocates are enthusiastic about you; they say all those good things about you that you would be embarrassed to say about yourself.

I've tried to help people get good jobs, political appointments, or elected to public office. I also have tried to get people into colleges; to get their articles published; and to get recognition for public service. The one thing I know above all else is this: There is no substitute for an advocate, that person who will go the extra mile for you; that person who will not quit; that person who puts your interests before his or her interests.

Your advocate will make things happen for you that you can't make happen for yourself. Your advocate will care about you. Your advocate won't let you fail even if you consider failing. Your advocate will keep telling you what Yogi Berra would tell you: "It ain't over until it's over."

Advocates lobby for you in all the ways that you can't for yourself. If you have an advocate helping you to get a job, you are in good shape. ". . no enemy can match a friend." (Jonathan Swift)

CHAPTER 14
MENTORS

If you are in a job and don't have a mentor, you should be cleaning out your desk. You won't make it up the ladder in business, government, or education without a mentor. In fact, you'll be lucky to even find the ladder.

The dictionary defines "mentor" as a "trusted friend or guide"; a "tutor or coach." I define mentor as the person who helps you to be successful in spite of yourself. We are, each of us, our own worst enemy. We constantly do dumb things that would be destructive but for friends and family. A mentor cares about you and helps you regardless of your "foolish" mistakes. Yet, strangely enough, many mentors do not know they're mentors—they're simply helping because they like you. Even stranger is the fact that many people who are helped by a mentor don't realize they have a mentor. They think they're "going places" on their own. Not a chance. If you're getting ahead, somebody is helping you.

I can recall virtually all my mentors in hindsight. At the time, I didn't know what they were other than people who occasionally helped me, even when I didn't deserve it.

I was graduated from high school on a Friday night and joined the Army the following Monday morning. I had been in the Army National Guard during high school and had decided on a military career. After completing advanced infantry training and airborne school, I was assigned to a rifle unit in the 82nd Airborne Division. I don't recall what happened to my military career, but I remember that I disliked the Army so much that I would have accepted a bad conduct discharge to get out. But that didn't happen. An older sergeant kept me out of the stockade, sent me to school, and generally watched over me. I made it for three years, one month and twenty-two days with a self-destructive attitude but without self-destructing. I made it because one sergeant cared for me. He helped me, yet, at the time, I didn't realize the value of his guidance. It would be years later before I understood.

I often think about the importance of my military mentor. Had it not been for him, I would have received less than an honorable discharge.

Without an honorable discharge, I would not have attended college, never would have gone to graduate school, and never would have gone to law school. I would not have qualified to be a registered stockbroker, or received a license to practice law, or have been considered for teaching appointments at prestigious colleges and universities. One person made the difference in the beginning of my career. Others have helped each me step of the way. They are mentors. We all have to have mentors and should be mentors.

As a young man starting out as a clerk in the stock brokerage business, I earned $1.25 an hour. Not much pay. But I had something better than pay. At least two senior partners in the firm encouraged me to stay in school, regularly saw to it that I had promotional opportunities, and provided me with the opportunity to study to become a registered stockbroker while I was attending school and working part-time. They were there for me with my hardly knowing it and certainly never appreciating it.

In my first teaching job after graduate school, a mentor kept me on track. In my first teaching job after law school, a mentor ensured that I was well received by other faculty. In my government job after teaching, I had a mentor who would listen to me complain about the agency's decisions and when I was finished, he would explain why I was wrong. He would spend hours with me discussing issues— tutoring, if you will—without saying I was stupid, a slow learner, hard-headed, etc. In short, he brought me along at my learning pace. In a few years, others credited me with being an expert in my field, but I gained my expertise by making stupid and erroneous arguments to someone who cared enough to teach me the correct arguments. He would never say I was wrong without explaining why. Even a hard- head like me can learn eventually, if someone keeps providing the right answers and explaining the logic behind them.

I spent a year working for one of the most prestigious corporations in America. The general counsel made certain I had every opportunity to advance. Amazingly, although I worked for the company for only a year, my mentor continues to recommend me.

What a wonderful experience to have someone you only worked for a year care about you all your professional life.

For the past seventeen years in private law practice, a senior partner in my firm has helped me, no matter what the circumstance. Sometimes he has tried a case for me; sometimes he has gotten a new client, collected a bill, listened to my wild ideas; or simply has been a friend. No matter what the ups and downs—and the downs in law practice can be very, very down—he has always been there. Without him, I could not have made it a month, certainly not almost three decades.

Every opportunity I have had arose because someone in a position to help me has helped me. If you don't have someone looking out for you in your job, you should move on. Others in the organization do have people looking out for them, tutoring them, providing assistance, and doing all these other things that create successful employment opportunities. They will succeed or at least have a realistic opportunity to succeed.

You may be young and not think about mentors or you may ask, "How do I know whether I have a mentor?" I only know about mentors in hindsight. But then I never asked myself, "Does someone in this company, agency, university, etc. want me to succeed?" If yes, is that person(s) in a position to help me? The only permanent job I have had in which I did not have a mentor was my Wall Street job. And I should have realized going in that I didn't have one. But I didn't

—and, as you know by now, I wasn't in the "Big Apple" long.

No one climbs the ladder of success alone. People are pulled up and they are pushed up. If people are not pulling and pushing you, you need to find another ladder to climb. No job mentor, no job momentum. If you don't have a mentor friend, find one. And remember, "… the only way to find a friend is to be one." (Ralph Waldo Emerson)

CHAPTER 15

SHOOT HIGH

I've been helping people with jobs for over twenty-five years. In that time, I have learned it's best to talk directly to top management about prospective employees than indirectly through a human resources manager or administrative assistants, secretaries, and others. Yet, quite frequently, I find myself talking to such individuals because it's easier than talking directly to the person at the top unless, of course, he or she is a personal friend.

Not long ago, I helped a friend enter private law practice after seventeen years in government service. My first step in assisting him was to find two people I knew who worked for the firm he was interested in joining. That's my usual modus operandi—find insiders whom I know well enough that I can get their help to help someone I'm trying to help. In this instance, I found two insiders who were willing to help and, in fact, their support for this particular friend was critical. They were powerful insiders in one of the top law firms in the country; their recommendation would be taken quite seriously and, indeed, probably not challenged unless economic or other similar reasons required otherwise. In speaking to the insiders about helping my friend, one gave me valuable advice. He reminded me that I knew the people at the top; they liked me; and they wouldn't want to turn me down unless, again, economic conditions required that response. Thus, he advised me to "shoot high" in my efforts. In fact, I was assured that there was no downside although I certainly didn't have the clout to make it happen for my friend.

In any event, I did just what I was told; I went to the top. And yes, they were very respectful and, no, they didn't hire my friend on my recommendation. But my recommendation was considered and at least it gave those at the top reason to pause before acting on my friend's application. And during the "pause" period—I'll call it the "incubation" period—my two insider friends were able to garner other internal support for my friend and, eventually, close the deal. The firm invited my friend to join their partnership. I can't take credit for my friend's relatively easy and successful entry into the private sector after seventeen years in federal and state governments. But I know my direct contact with the law firm's top management didn't hurt. Indeed, I am convinced that I probably caused a pause that allowed the "movers and shakers" on the inside to make it happen.

Why after all these years of helping others in their job search was I reluctant to go directly to the top to help a friend? I don't know the answer, but I know now that I shouldn't be reluctant. People at the top of most organizations are usually very respectful of others' judgment, and if they know you, they will at least hear you out. If you have the opportunity to make a pitch to the boss on behalf of a friend, make it. "Only those who will risk going too far can possibly find out how far one can go." (T.S. Elliott)

In another instance, I was supporting a very bright young woman to succeed to the head of a government agency. I knew she was exceptionally qualified; I had worked closely with her and knew the extent of her job skills. I did something I had never done before. I personally telephoned several of the agency's board of directors to ask for their support. On the one hand, I felt very strongly that she was the perfect person to lead the agency—an agency that badly needed credibility. She had all the qualifications—credibility, experience, business and critical thinking skills. Equally important, she is a great people person, a desperately needed skill at the agency. On the other hand, I was concerned that my lobbying would be viewed by the board as meddling and, thus, hurt her chances. Boards often don't like outsiders telling them who to hire. Regardless, she got the job, and my lobbying was not considered meddling. I "shot high" and it helped.

What I learned from these two experiences is that friends are probably reluctant to go directly to the top of an organization to help friends with jobs. They fear, as I feared, that they will be embarrassed and/or it will hurt instead of helping a friend's chances. But the truth is that people at the top are respectful of the opinions of others even if they're only acquaintances. Most importantly, they're not going to penalize an acquaintance for trying to help a friend. So take the shot. For he "who shoots at the midday sun, though he be sure he shall never hit the mark, yet as sure he is he shall shoot higher than he who aims but at a bush." (New Arcadia [1590], 2)

CHAPTER 16
BOTHERSOME PEOPLE

The typical caller seeking job advice is unhappy with his or her employment. But, invariably, it is not the job. It is the people with whom they work. The usual complaint is that a manager or fellow worker is selfish—he or she wants all the credit for the work or they refuse to acknowledge the good work of the caller. Another usual complaint is that a boss will not provide a challenging environment. Another is that the people around them are "back biters."

Such people believe that by simply changing jobs things will be better. While that may be true, there is probably just as good a chance that they will not be better off in a new job. Unfortunately, every employee, including top management, has to deal with people with whom they would rather not. As a lawyer, I frequently deal with clients with whom I would rather not. In fact, if the truth be known, most lawyers probably consider their clients a "pain in the butt." They make an infinite number of demands and then complain about the lawyer's bill because he or she billed too much time doing, guess what? You guessed it: responding to the client's demands.

The point is not that clients are difficult; the point is that every work environment involves working with a few difficult people. Some, of course, are more difficult than others, but it is inescapable that we all have to deal with such people. Does changing your job solve the problem? Of course not. Again, it is just as likely that you will encounter people in your new job who irritate you as "much" as the people in your former job. Thus, in changing jobs, you may be "jumping out of the frying pan into the fire."

Interestingly, although interpersonal relationships are a prime motivation for many who change jobs, people don't try to find out about the people in a new job until after they're on the job. It's a strange phenomenon, yet typical.

Change jobs because you want to do another job; change jobs to rekindle the creative talents in you; change jobs because you want to be near your parents, near your children, or near your church. Change jobs because you want to live in the mountains or near the water. But don't change jobs because you don't like some of the people with whom you work. You may be able to get away with it once or twice, but you shouldn't make a habit of it because you would quickly develop a reputation as the one who has the problem

—not the people you leave behind. You become the one with the dubious reputation even if your former coworkers were indeed "pains in the butt." And you never want that to happen. "Be it true or false, what is said about men often has as much influence upon their lives, and especially upon their destinies, as what they do." (Victor Hugo)

CHAPTER 17

COLD CALLING

I rank cold calling for jobs right up there with selling refrigerators to Eskimos. Cold calling can work, but it is a hard road and it requires considerable luck. Imagine finding an Eskimo with no ice but electricity. That's about how lucky you will have to be to find a job by cold calling.

That is not to say that you can't find jobs by making cold calls. I made a cold call on the U.S. Army and was hired (much to my surpise). I secured teaching jobs in Virginia and Ohio by writing colleges where I had no contacts. They were cold calls; the jobs I found were also entry-level jobs. Admittedly, cold calling did result in my getting a relatively good job in New York, namely, the Wall Street job I mentioned in chapter 2. Inasmuch as I had been in the stockbrokerage industry—and had done quite well, thank you—I assumed that I could go door to door on Wall Street and find a good job. After all, I had experience; I had been successful; and I had an MBA (which not everybody had in the late 1960s).

Much to my chagrin, most stockbrokerage firms in New York at the time gave new broker candidates intelligence and psychological tests. To say that I do not test well is an understatement. In my first half-dozen Wall Street interviews, I barely made the cut. I probably qualified for jobs, but I certainly was not considered a top candidate. Regardless, I kept knocking on doors; I kept taking tests, tests, and more tests. Eventually, guess what happened? I became an "expert test taker" of the tests administered by the prestigious Wall Street firms.

By the time I got to the door of one of the most prominent stockbrokerage firms on Wall Street, I knew the tests the firms were giving and the answers the tests usually required. I was ready to be tested. As it happened, I did not need to be well prepared. The test I was given did not require a lot of skill. It was the same test that I had taken several days before at another brokerage firm. (They probably use the same consultants who charge twice for doing the same job.)

In any event, I was hired as the new "superstar" because of my success in my prior job as a stockbroker and, also, my "high intellect." I had greatly impressed my new employers with my excellent test score.

Notwithstanding their high expectations, the Dow Jones Industrial Average was at 600+ (compared to reaching 10,000 plus in 2000) and no one was buying stocks, and if they were, they certainly weren't buying from me. Six months later, I was U-hauling it to Virginia with a wife six months pregnant. The only type of employment test I have taken since my Wall Street ventures is the bar examination; it was certainly clear to the bar examiners that I was no superstar. I made the cut—but, I expect, barely.

It is true that some people do get good jobs by cold calling. But, again, it's usually a result of luck and certainly is not as efficient as locating a job with the help of friends and family. The odds of landing a job from making cold calls are simply too high. For most good jobs, there are dozens, if not hundreds, of applicants. Even if you are highly qualified, there are others equally qualified. Cold calling is simply playing the odds—odds that are not very good. The people you're competing with have their friends trying to help them; some have their own advocates making calls behind the scenes; and some even have political help.

Again, selling refrigerators in Alaska or cold calling is a long shot. I have tried the latter but not the former. I would try the former before I would go cold calling again for a job. But, if you must make cold calls, remember what Benjamin Franklin said: "He that can have patience can have what he will."

I have only one theory that has worked to help friends get political appointments. It's called "preemption."

I have helped a half dozen or so friends obtain high-level government jobs—otherwise called political appointments. In some instances, the jobs were significant promotions for the friends. In other instances, they were new appointments in agencies other than those in which the friends worked. In virtually every case, the only strategy that I have found to work is to "preempt" the field; i.e., lock up a job before anyone knows about it.

For most high-level government jobs, one can expect a significant number of applications. I am currently assisting a friend to find such a job as I write this book, and I am having a difficult time. He asked for my help after the government job he is seeking had been advertised for several months. By the time I got involved, there were over 200 applicants for that job. It took letters and telephone calls from me and several other friends to executives at the government agency to ensure that he even got an interview. Unfortunately, six other candidates were interviewed. He is well qualified for the job and may yet get it, but his prospects are no better than 50/50 at best. It is best to avoid head-to-head competition among equally qualified candidates for such jobs. If you know of a top-level government job, or have a friend seeking such a job, garner the support of the people who have the most interest in who gets the job before there is significant interest in the job. If the main players are on board, and you have a good candidate, you can often short-circuit the entire process and ensure that the job is never opened up to the world at large.

I usually do not know the right people who can help friends get high-level government jobs. But I often know someone who knows someone who knows someone else who knows someone else. Most people will get on board quickly to help a qualified candidate obtain a high-level position, particularly if they have an interest in who fills that position. Restaurants, for example, have an interest in who is on the Alcoholic Beverage Control Board. Likewise, industrialists and environmentalists have an interest in who is appointed to the air board; electric utilities have an interest in who is appointed director of energy regulation at the state public utilities commission; bankers have an interest in who is appointed commissioner of banking; and insurance companies who have an interest in who is appointed commissioner of insurance. The key is to identify those who have an interest (i.e., the stakeholders) in seeing who gets a particular job and get them interested in your candidate before other candidates apply.

How do you get such key players as allies? One simple method is to have the stakeholders make phone calls to the persons in charge of the hiring. That, however, is a risky strategy because different messages will get delivered by the different stakeholders. A better approach is to have highly reputable members of the community sign a letter in support of a candidate, particularly if they know and can discuss his or her background and qualifications. If you can get community leaders to support a candidate, and to send the same message, and the candidate has the right background and qualifications, you're virtually assured of success. You get the right candidate for the right job; you save the bureaucracy the time and expense of advertising and interviewing; and, most importantly, you end up with a known product. Nobody would like to take the chance that a high-level government position is filled by a "kook." When reputable people make recommendations about someone they know, it makes the selection process easy. Having community leaders backing a particular candidate keeps other candidates out of the hunt. Get community leaders involved early, and you will lap the field. "For the strength of the Pack is the Wolf, and the strength of the Wolf is the Pack." (Rudyard Kipling, the "Law of the Jungle")

CHAPTER 19

JOB POLITICS

How many times have you heard someone say that this person or that person got his or her job or promotion because of politics? Similar refrains include: "He is part of the 'good old boy network' "; "they're fellow jocks"; "they're fraternity brothers"; "they're members of the same country club"; or "they're first families"; "blue blood." Worst yet, you hear that he or she "brown noses" or "kisses butt" or whatever. At best, these are claims that politics played a major role in a job or job promotion. At worst, they are implications that the person being talked about did not get his or her job on the basis of merit.

We are all probably guilty of making statements to the effect that someone, somewhere, got his or her job because of politics. You may not have made such a statement outright but you have probably thought it. Why? In part, it's a defensive mechanism to explain why we haven't done as well in our jobs. If we could be objective about this issue (and we can't), we would probably conclude that nobody gets his job or promotion solely because of politics. However, there is probably some political influence in virtually all jobs and promotions, including ours.

In my law practice, I would regularly appear before government agencies. Invariably, I was asked by clients whether I have the right "politics" to win a case. In other words, am I connected? My response for over thirty years has been that to win you have to be 100% right on the law, 100% right on the facts, and only then do you worry about the politics. That is not to say that politics aren't important; politics are important. But I doubt if politics alone ever work. In my experience, the people who win cases get jobs, promotions and otherwise are successful, qualified people. Politics play a role only after people are deemed qualified.

In early 1997, I was involved in the selection of someone for an administrative job in the firm. The person I promoted for the job had been highly recommended to me by a friend whose judgment I highly regard. Therefore, I relied on his judgment in recommending this particular candidate over another equally qualified candidate. Some might say that the person I promoted got her job because of politics (she knew someone). And it's hard to disagree with the facts. She knew someone (my friend) who knew someone (me) and that connection made the difference in her getting the job. However, she was certainly qualified.

There is no question that it pays to know someone. But knowing someone will seldom get you a job unless you are qualified for the job to begin with. I have helped many people find jobs or get promotions because of my friendship with them or my friendship with others who knew them, but I can't recall a single instance when the person was not qualified for the job or even not as qualified as the leading candidate for the job.

True, a job or promotion doesn't happen without some politics. But you must make certain that the qualifications and job match before utilizing your connections. The worst of all worlds is to waste political capital trying to get someone a job to which he or she isn't suited. It won't work and after a while you will exhaust your political capital. Friends will always be there for you, but political help is here today and gone tomorrow. Don't squander a valuable political resource without at least having a realistic chance at a job. In short, use politics, but use it wisely. "The whole art of politics consists in directing rationally the irrationalities of men." (Attributed to Reinhold Niebuhr)

CHAPTER 20

RÉSUMÉ HELP

I despair every time I see a résumé. I know that virtually everyone's first step in looking for a job, or in seeking a promotion, is to prepare or revise his or her résumé. I know that hours of work go into résumé preparation; I know that an impressive résumé is important to the person whose name is on it. People probably feel the same way about their résumés as they do about their appearance. They probably feel that the appearance of their résumé can somehow make a difference in others' evaluation of them.

All I can say about the extra effort that goes into résumé preparation is "bunk." Résumés are like underwear. We feel that we need spiffy-looking underwear. But no matter how attractive our underwear, the appearance has little meaning to others (assuming that most people are not seen in their underwear). Bluntly put, I don't believe that a fancy résumé has much to do with your getting a job.

Why do the résumé preparers and revisers put in all that work? Employers get names, addresses, and telephone numbers from résumés and make some preliminary judgment about qualifications; they input the data in the computer and then file the résumé. A résumé is basic information to prospective employers. If they are looking for a person with a degree in electrical engineering and five years of electrical engineering experience, the résumé gets your name on the list of people responding to an ad with a degree in electrical engineering and five years of electrical engineering experience. It doesn't get you the job; it doesn't get you an interview; it could get you a phone call and an interview if the information on the résumé matches the background and qualifications that the employer is seeking.

Yes, I confess I have spent a lot of time revising my résumé. In fact, I am embarrassed to admit it, but I revise my résumé almost every month (I call it "updating"). Thus, you ask: Why does he do it and tell me not to do it? The answer is simple: for the same reason other people spend an inordinate amount of time preparing and revising their résumé. They didn't finish college or graduate from an Ivy League school, or even graduate from a regional prep college. They know many people who went to "better schools." They (and I) therefore try to make up for such inadequacies by "beefing up" their (my) résumé. It's natural behavior. We want to try and look better than we actually are. There's nothing wrong with that.

But it should be obvious. "Beefing up" a résumé isn't going to get you a better job than you would have otherwise gotten. I didn't graduate from Harvard, but I have spent years "beefing up" my résumé. And guess what? I still don't have a Harvard degree on my résumé. In fact, after decades of revising my résumé (and even having it edited by some exceptionally qualified writers), I find that the information is still basically the same. I received an undergraduate degree from a local college with no honors (that's short for I barely made it); I received an MBA from a business school that I couldn't get into now; I received a law degree without distinction from an elite law school, but the only reason I got in was because the younger brother of the dean of admissions was one of my best childhood friends.

I have tried every conceivable way to make my credentials seem comparable to those of truly accomplished people; but, when all is said and done, I am what I am. No matter what we put on our résumés, we can't change the facts. The facts are what they are; we are who we are.

What then should be the objective in preparing a résumé? The answer is "KISS" (keep it simple, stupid). Put down your name, address, telephone number, education, and employment history. If you feel compelled to embellish your résumé, add a few sentences describing particular employment experiences.

But spending hours trying to make yourself look like the greatest data processing clerk who ever worked for K-Mart is useless. Few employers will care about how great you describe yourself on your résumé. They will check out your references; they will check on your skills. What they need to know from your résumé is that you have the requisite background and experience.

I believe a résumé should be like a calling card. It should provide your name, address, telephone number, education, and experience.

If a prospective employer wants to know more after you have given them your "calling card," he will ask. Writing more on a calling card isn't helpful. Lengthy résumés aren't helpful. "There are some circumstances in life where truth and simplicity are the best strategy in the world." (Jean de La Bruyere, French moralist) Writing a résumé is one of those circumstances.

CHAPTER 21

REHEARSING

Rehearsing is a word that conjures up memories of weddings or school plays. We don't usually think of rehearsing in connection with jobs. But why not? If it is necessary for people to rehearse a wedding just so they know where to stand, surely it is necessary to rehearse for a job interview.

People, of course, rehearse for weddings because they are fun, particularly for the bride's parents who finally get to do something without having to pick up a tab. That's fun. Rehearsing for a job interview is not fun. In fact, most job seekers I have known didn't rehearse for interviews. That is amazing. Anyone asked to perform in a play or participate in a wedding would assume that rehearsing is necessary. Why? To get it right. Yet, for reasons that are a mystery to me, people don't think it is necessary to rehearse for a job interview.

I have practiced law for over 30 years and taught college or law school full time or part time for 30 years. I couldn't go to court on the simplest matter without an outline and rehearsing what I'm going to say. I can't even go to a class that I've taught for two decades without preparation. How then could I ever go to a job interview without preparation? Of course, I couldn't. I'm not that smart. Maybe others are. But I think they're inviting failure. To quote a former UCLA head coach of basketball, John Wooden, "Failure to prepare is preparing to fail."

Almost any interviewer interviewing a prospective employee is going to be asking basic questions such as: "Why do you want to work here?" "What do you know about us?" "What are your background and relevant experience?" "Why are you leaving your present job?" "What are your goals and objectives?" These are not questioning only a "rocket scientist" can answer. But they still require preparation to give satisfactory answers.

When my older daughter was interviewing for a bank job, I collected annual reports from her targeted banks for her review so that she would at least know the sizes of her targeted banks, which states they operate in, how many branches they each have and so on. Very basic information yet, in my judgment, very important information. If an interviewer asks:

"What do you know about us?" and your only response is "You're a bank," I think you're in trouble.

I once asked a prospective secretary what she knew about my law firm. She gave a quick answer: "Lawyers work here." *Wow*, I thought. *And I am supposed to turn over critical client work to her?* Not a chance.

Rehearsing for an interview is not difficult. You can have a friend ask you a few basic questions, particularly a friend who knows something about the company and/or the job. This is a brief exercise that you will find invaluable. Any true friend will meet you for lunch or coffee and ask you questions to see how well you respond. This is a must, no matter what your level of experience.

I once assisted a former legislator in his efforts to obtain an important government job. One of the things he had to do to secure the job was to be interviewed by a legislative panel. This individual had over twenty years experience serving in the legislature and knew everyone on the panel, yet, when I asked him to go over his remarks and answer some questions in preparation for his interview, he agreed without blinking. He understood the value of preparation.

Preparation is especially important as you move up the job ladder. People doing the interviewing want to hear something worthwhile so they can evaluate you. It might be a statement expressing how you intend to operate a division or department; it might be your vision for the division or department; it might be a description of your management style; it might be how you intend to accomplish your goals and objectives; it might be about anything. And for you to discuss something well requires preparation—at least it does for most of us.

What then is the most valuable preparation? After all, you could be asked anything. It's hard to anticipate everything. Well, for certain, you should be able to answer who, what, where, and when; that is, who you are; what your background and experience are; when you decided to change jobs and why; and where you see yourself in five years, ten years, and so on. If you can't answer these basic questions, you're not going to get a mail clerk's job. But aside from the who, what, when, and where, what are other likely important questions you'll be asked? Obviously, I can't answer that question because I don't know which job you are seeking and, even if I did, I wouldn't know what a particular company is looking for. But I can tell you a lesson that I learned in my first job in the stockbrokerage business, and I have never forgotten it. It has served me well in court, teaching, job interviews, and, in fact, in appearances before virtually any group. The advice is as stable as the Rock of Gibraltar: "If you see Jimmy Jones through Jimmy Jones' eyes, you'll sell Jimmy Jones what Jimmy Jones buys."

The "Jimmy Jones advice" is sound and will endure. Know what your interviewer wants and give it to him. Tell him what he wants to hear—not what you want to tell him. When you think about it, that's really the difference between students who do well and those who do not. Students who do well quickly figure out what the teacher is trying to get him or her to learn. You could be a brilliant student and give teachers brilliant answers, but you're in trouble if you're not giving them the answers for which they are looking.

In a job interview, you must make enough inquiries to at least find out what a company is looking for, i.e., what is it that the interviewer wants to hear. If you do that, "you'll see Jimmy Jones through Jimmy Jones' eyes and you'll sell Jimmy Jones what Jimmy Jones buys." If you insist on telling Jimmy Jones what you want to tell him, you should also plan on telling him good-bye. "Two great talkers will not travel far together." (Spanish proverb)

CHAPTER 22
REFERENCES

I have been used as a reference for my former secretaries and former colleagues, government officials, other lawyers, educators, consultants, and others. The one thing I know with absolute certainty is that references count—and they count for a lot. Yet, surprisingly, people spend almost no time talking to or even thinking about their references. Typically, we include on our résumé a statement that references are "available upon request." Who are they? They're available for what? To say what? We don't know because we assume our references ("players to be named later") will say all the right things. Wrong! They will say what they think are the right things to say. Whether the things they say are helpful to us depends largely on luck!

If you intend to use someone as a reference, you need to spend time with the person telling him or her about your job prospects, your interests and, equally importantly, any particular problems that you have had locating a job. It is foolish to start looking for a job and not have your references lined up and knowledgeable about you and why you are looking. The more they know, the better off you are.

It is truly amazing that we give such little information to our references. Any reference you think enough of to list as a reference will certainly try to help. That goes without saying. But he or she can't help if he or she doesn't know enough about you. For example, I was listed as a reference for a fine young man who had the perfect credentials for a job in the environmental field. Everything seemed on track for him to get the position. At the interview, however, he became extremely anxious— even to the point of breaking out in tears. This had the effect of raising doubts about his ability to speak to groups, which was necessary in the job. Fortunately, I knew the reasons for his nervousness. First, he had been unemployed for two years and had lost his confidence. Second, he had recently lost his father. The combination made him less confident than the interviewers had expected, given his impressive background and experience. When I was called and asked about his nervous condition, I readily agreed that he was anxious to the extent of creating the impression that it was a permanent condition. But I explained that I thought it was quite natural for anyone who had been unemployed for two years and who had recently lost a parent not to convey the confidence that others might in an interview. I had known the individual for enough years to believe that with his reemployment, especially reemployment in his field, he would regain his confidence. I knew that because I knew him. I also knew exactly what the caller was talking about when he called because I had met a number of times with the individual in question and, in the process of discussing his job prospects, I detected his anxiety. It was obvious. Indeed, the longer he was unemployed, the more anxious he became. His condition was understandable.

In any event, the point should be obvious. A reference who knows a job candidate and what he's been through for the last couple of years is able to give interviewers a plausible explanation, and, in my example, an explanation that was critical in allaying the prospective employer's concerns. The anxious young man was hired and is performing beautifully in his new job. Had I not known enough about the individual's loss of confidence because of his lengthy unemployment and about the loss of his parent, I would not have had a helpful explanation for the interviewers.

In another instance, being an informed reference was similarly critical. I recommended a young woman for a senior position in government. The department head was concerned about her background and experience. She was exceptionally strong in one particular area but weak in another. Strengths in both areas were required for the job. In my opinion, however, her strengths more than outweighed her weaknesses, but that's not easy to explain. Fortunately, I knew her well enough as an individual to know that she would be a wonderful manager. She had that certain charisma that made people around her enthusiastic about working with her. She is a person you want to work with and help in her job. She is not simply someone you are satisfied to work for. Because I knew this person's personality strengths, I was absolutely confident that she could overcome any particular weaknesses. And because of my confidence in and knowledge of her, I was able to explain how her strengths outweighed her weaknesses. She would excel beyond expectations where she had strengths; she would also excel beyond expectations where she had weaknesses because the people working with her would give her exceptional support. My knowledge of her strengths and weaknesses, I believe, was critical to her getting the job.

In another instance, I was asked by a "headhunter," or executive search firm, to list an individual's strengths and weaknesses. Again, I was fortunate to know enough about the individual to give a genuine and complete response with sufficient particularities that the headhunter knew that I knew what I was talking about. It's easy to say he or she is a great person, has a wonderful personality, is industrious, and so on. But you have to know someone to declare that they're organized, whether they would macro-manage or micro- manage, whether they motivate or demoralize people, whether they are tenacious, dedicated, and so on. Also, explaining peoples' strengths and weaknesses with examples, I think, makes a reference more effective. With respect to my last example though, I had to tell the headhunter that I did not know of any weaknesses, except that he ate too much pasta. Apparently it didn't hurt my friend's job prospect.

A final thought about references. I have frequently been asked by employers calling about former employees of my firm, including lawyers and secretaries, whether I would re-hire the person. If I can state that I would without equivocation, I answer, "absolutely yes." If I am in doubt, I refer the caller to our personnel department. I don't know what happens after that. But I do know that being able to tell another employer that I would rehire a former employee has as great an impact as anything else I could tell someone calling for a reference. In fact, this is such common sense it would seem that everyone would make certain that when they leave a job, there is someone with the former employer who will state unequivocally that the departing employee would be rehired. If your former employer has the slightest bit of queasiness about giving you a solid reference, you had better get the reason for the queasy feeling resolved. "To have lost your reputation is to be dead among the living."
(S.H. Simmons)

CHAPTER 23

WANT AD HELP

I doubt if many people reading this book have read more want ads than I have read. I am fifty-nine years old at the time of the publication of this book, and I have been reading want ads in several newspapers on a regular basis since 1962. You might recall in chapter 12 that I was reading the want ads on a Sunday morning at the beach when I found the perfect job match for a friend I'd been trying to help for several years.

Putting my interest aside, the question is how likely are you to find a job from a want ad? The answer, I think, depends more on the level of the job than anything else. Entry-level jobs can be found in the want ads; however, you will never get a high-level job from a want ad. High-level jobs will go to friends of friends or will be filled by headhunters. Middle-level jobs from want ads—maybe, but probably not.

Why then do I read want ads? Simple. I am an addicted job searcher. I really don't expect to find a job for myself or for friends in want ads. Indeed, I can tell you countless stories about jobs advertised that were filled before the ad was even placed. More often than not, a good job is advertised because regulations of some sort require advertisement but, in plain truth, there is someone already lined up for the job. Good jobs are filled long before they are generally known—or at least friends have gotten friends lined up for the job and ahead of the pack, so to speak.

Having stated my reservation about want ads, I would add that ads are still a good starting point if you are looking for an entry-level job, a sales job, or a summer job. Even if I didn't believe (and I don't) that you have a good chance of finding an executive job in the want ads, I would still read the want ads to keep myself informed about the job market, salary levels, and the type of jobs that are advertised in a particular area. You can get a good indication of how robust the job market is from want ads.

You also get information about which companies in the area are hiring and the ones that are not.

In short, read the want ads while you are waiting for friends to return your phone calls; read the want ads while waiting in the doctor's office; read the want ads while standing in line in the grocery store; read the want ads while waiting for a pick-up. Just don't do it when you have something important to do unless, of course, you're desperate for any type of job. If you are, don't be ashamed. "There is no labor a man can do that's undignified if he does it right." (*Unknown*)

CHAPTER 24

DOWN AND OUT

Do you have a friend who's been looking for a job for six months, a year, or even more? Do you have a friend who's been "downsized" (a.k.a. "laid off")? I have had such friends; in fact, it has happened to me. These are painful, miserable situations. And the misery only gets worse with every day of unemployment.

The longer a person goes without a job, the more difficult it becomes to find a job. There are two reasons for that. First, employers always seem to want someone who is already employed, *i.e.*, in demand. For whatever reason, unemployed people seem less valuable than employed people. I suspect there is little empirical evidence to support this notion, but, who cares what the evidence shows? It's a fact of life. Employers are simply not as enthusiastic about unemployed prospects as they are about employed prospects. Second, the longer one goes unemployed and the more one receives rejections, the harder it seems to sell oneself. To begin with, employers aren't usually looking for unemployed people. Equally important, the longer one remains unemployed, the more he or she feels rejected. The more he/she feels rejected, the harder it is to present him/herself as a "dynamic overachiever"; in fact, the harder it is to sell oneself as even an "underachiever." True, I have no training in psychology, but this is common sense. It also has happened to me. I have had prolonged periods of unemployment. It isn't easy; and things surely seem to get worse long before they seem to get better.

How then do you help someone who is "down and out"? How do you help yourself when you're down and out? Obviously, there is no single or simple answer. Yet, there is an answer that has consistently worked for me—indeed, for over forty years. When I'm down and out about a job—I'm out. In other words, I get out. At age eighteen, I intended to make the military a career, but it didn't work. I was dejected about my experience. I got out at age twenty-one and tried making a career in the small-loan business. That didn't work either. I started working in the stockbrokerage business and attending college.

I became a registered stockbroker but, later, when that didn't work, I started over again by going to graduate school. After graduate school, I went back into the stockbrokerage business, and when that didn't work, I started over again in teaching. And when that didn't work, I started over again by going to law school.

After law school, I tried teaching again. When that didn't work, I tried government, and when government work lost its appeal for me, I found work with a corporation. After a year of corporate work, I decided to change to private law practice.

I know it's easier to say you'll start over than actually doing it; I know it's particularly difficult when you have a spouse and children. But I also know that you can't do what you don't try. A colleague once gave me a quote that he attributed to a great hockey player, Wayne Gretzky. It's a great saying: "You miss 100% of the shots you never take." I remember that during the last days of my military career I was restricted to the barracks for being "absent without leave (AWOL)." That's the bad news. The good news is that I took that opportunity to read Norman Vincent Peale's *The Power of Positive Thinking*. He changed me from a pessimist to an optimist: "No matter how dark things seem to be or actually are, raise your sights and see the possibilities—always see them, for they're always there."

If you're down and out, or if you have a friend who's down and out, and all else fails, start over. Start a new career; attend school; join the military; start your own small business; go into sales; start at the bottom of the family business; rake leaves; paint houses. Use your imagination. "Imagination is more important than knowledge." (Albert Einstein)

I once had an acquaintance who was a professional human resources employee of a large company. The company let him go. When he couldn't find employment after some time, he started driving a truck. He did it well; he saved money; later, he opened his own executive recruitment office.

Starting over gives people a new lease on life. Starting over can open doors for opportunities that you never dreamed of, much less thought you could have. Anybody can start over. People can make you feel down and out, but they can't stop you from starting over—no matter what your age, occupation, race, or gender. "It's not whether you get knocked down, it's whether you get up." (Vince Lombardi)

You shouldn't tell former employers to "take this job and shove it" because you never know when you'll be back or need their recommendation. Nevertheless, you can start anew if you think you can:

If you think you are beaten, you are; If you think you dare not, you don't. If you'd like to win, but think you can't, It's almost a cinch you won't. If you think you'll lose, you're lost, For out in the world we find Success begins with a fellow's will; It's all in the state of mind. If you think you're outclassed, you are; You've got to think high to rise. You've got to be sure of yourself before You can ever win a prize. Life's battles don't always go To the stronger or faster man; But soon or late the man who wins Is the one who thinks he can.

Walter A. Wintle, "The Man Who Thinks He Can," *Poems That Live Forever,* comp. Hazel Felleman, p. 310 (1965)

CHAPTER 25

GET A PLAN: GUT IT OUT

I know people who have spent their entire life looking for the right job; in fact, I'm one of them. I've been a paratrooper, small-loan officer, stockbroker, college professor, and lawyer. As a stockbroker, I worked for three different stockbrokerage firms; as a college professor, I have taught full time at four universities and part time at six universities. As a lawyer, I have worked for the government, a corporation, and in private practice with two major law firms. I'm still on the lookout for new part-time and full-time employment opportunities.

Looking for a job, particularly the right job, can be discouraging, no question about it. And that's true even if you've never been unemployed. But I don't look at job hunting negatively. No matter what the job, or what the circumstances surrounding an existing job, I look for new opportunities because I believe that everyone can find better opportunities if he wants to badly enough.

Why I am persistent in my job search and why I encourage others to be the same is because it keeps me enthusiastic. It keeps me enthusiastic about my present job because if I decide to leave, I certainly want to leave with a good attitude. It keeps me enthusiastic about the future because I see almost unlimited opportunities for everyone, including myself.

Of course, talk is cheap. It's easy to talk about better opportunities. And most people are too bogged down in their daily routine to dedicate themselves to job hunting. It's easy for me because I do it as a hobby. I certainly understand that not everyone reads the want ads as a hobby. But there are approaches to finding new opportunities and they're not time consuming. You simply have to be systematic in your approach. You can spend twenty minutes a week looking for a new job and eventually your persistence will pay off. All you need is a game plan. For example, find out how most jobs in your field become known. Are they posted on an electronic bulletin board? Are they noticed on a job hotline? Are they posted internally before being posted publicly? Do they appear principally in one publication? Are they the type of jobs that are advertised by word of mouth and, if yes, whose mouths; i.e., who tells the public about the jobs?

Every type of job in the world is filled from either a formal or informal process and usually both. While dozens of different processes may be used by some major corporations, most only use a couple of placement services or recruitment processes. Whatever the employment notification process, become informed as to what's available. Once you're in the pipeline—and it may be as simple as reading the classified section in an inter-office newspaper or in a trade publication—you will become knowledgeable about what jobs are out there in your area of interest, what they pay, and when they become available.

If you have your eyes and ears open and you know what you're looking for, and you know where to look, you will eventually hear of a better job opportunity. Whether you succeed in getting a job is another matter. That's where your background and experience, in addition to help from your friends, all come together. But you won't have the opportunity unless you have a plan to become informed about jobs in your area of interest. If you have a plan, and if you gut it out, it will all come together. I've seen it happen over and over. I love it when a plan comes together.

"Gutting it out" is a phrase familiar to the military. Making it through Marine boot camp requires "gutting it out." Making it through airborne training in the Army requires "gutting it out." People who go through such training usually have a plan, although they may not think of it as a plan at that particular time. It could be something as simple as being determined to always do one more push-up than the guy in front of you or beside you. If he makes it, you'll make it. It could be as simple as consistently cheering for your buddy because you know that he will cheer for you. He needs to be pumped up to make it; you need to be pumped up to make it.

But "gutting it out" doesn't just apply to the military. If you're recovering from a serious injury, "gutting it out" sometimes means taking one step more each day than you took the day before. Or if you're trying to quit drinking, it means one less glass of beer or wine at dinner until you've succeeded. Most people know what it means to "gut it out." In one way or another, we've all had objectives, and to accomplish our objectives, we've had to have a plan and "gut it out." There's no secret on how to "gut it out." The secret is how to make yourself do it.

If you're employed and you are looking to improve employment opportunities, develop a plan and "gut it out." In other words, make yourself stick to it. It won't be as hard as you think and you'll be proud of yourself when you do. Indeed, you will feel so accomplished that, I suspect, you will do it all over again in your next job and over again in the job after that one.

For the unemployed, "gutting it out" has an entirely different meaning. When you're unemployed and say you intend to "gut it out," what you mean is that you intend to make it; you intend to get back to work. The alternative to not "gutting it out" is not to make it. Given that there is no free lunch, if you're unemployed, you either "gut it out" in your job search or you join the ranks of the homeless. That's not a pleasant choice; that's the only choice.

For the unemployed, it's back to basics. Get yourself in the job market, develop a systematic plan, and stick to it. Your plan will work, and if it doesn't, modify the plan. What won't work is having no plan. Without a plan, there's nothing to stick to—there's nothing to "gut out."

I don't remember all of the clients I've had in my professional career, but I remember a few quite vividly. Some I remember for the wrong reason. What they did to others eventually got done to them, good or bad. Nothing is more true in life in general and in the business world in particular. It also is true that opportunity is the intersection of persistence and luck. People don't have successful lives without good luck. But good luck doesn't happen without hard work. "I'm a great believer in luck, and I find the harder I work the more I have of it." (Thomas Jefferson)

Develop a plan; stick to it. "Character consists of what you do on the third and fourth tries." (James Michener in
Chesapeake)

CHAPTER 26

LITTLE THINGS COUNT

The "little things" you do can make a big difference to a friend in need of a job. As a friend, you can help by making a telephone call to introduce your friend to persons in positions to hire or to assist with the employment process; you can write a letter on his or her behalf; or you can arrange a face-to-face meeting to introduce your friend to a prospective employer. These are neither difficult nor time-consuming tasks. Yet, they have the potential to change the life of your friend forever. You may recall in chapter 4 the account of my introduction of a Tennessee banker friend to a Virginia banker friend. The introduction involved nothing more than a telephone call. Yet, that call was the genesis of my Tennessee banker friend's new and highly successful banking career in Virginia.

You also may recall the incident in Ohio when I mentioned the background and qualifications of a professor friend in Virginia to a professor in Ohio. That brief introduction over lunch was a little thing. Yet, it helped launch my Virginia friend's highly successful career in education.

I've made calls simply to inquire about job openings and passed on the information to friends looking for jobs. I regularly check want ads and pass on information to job seekers when I see jobs that I think fit their background and experience. These are not difficult tasks, nor are they time consuming. Indeed, they're fun things to do that can also make a great difference to a friend in need of a job.

When it comes to writing letters of introduction or recommendations on behalf of friends or others, I will admit that that particular activity is more than just a little thing. It is important and it can be time consuming. But I have learned how to compose a knowledgeable letter of recommendation for a friend. I ask the friend to jot down notes about his or her background, experience and personal qualities. I particularly ask them about their major attributes and successes. For example, I might ask a secretary to describe how she organized files that had not been organized for years, or a salesman to describe how he was able to develop new clients, or an office manager to describe how he increased the efficiency and productivity of his office.

Having written notes in hand with specific information about a friend's accomplishments can considerably increase the substance of my letter of recommendation. The letter, of course, will say all the right (positive) things about my friend. But prospective employers are aided by specific information. Make such letters more meaningful by making them specific. Of course, your letters of recommendation must be truthful. Get the facts from your friend and write what you believe and know. It does not take much extra effort, but it would make a great difference to the reader; in fact, it could make all the difference in the world.

There are other small things that count. Personal introductions of your friend to a prospective employer that you know often make a great impact in the job search process. It does not require a lot of effort, but your personal interest will ensure that your employer friend will at least give your job-seeking friend reasonable consideration.

Another small thing that could make a huge difference is getting your spouse involved in the friend's job search if she can make a difference. Sometimes my wife knows an employer friend better than I do. If so, I ask her to write a note or make a phone call for my job-seeking friend. My wife never minds, and it's often a more effective letter or call than those I write on law-firm stationery. There are other advantages to having a spouse write or call. I write or call prospective employers all the time about friends and acquaintances who are looking for jobs. My wife doesn't. She is a preschool teacher, a mother of two daughters, and caretaker of her mother. "Jobs" is not a subject on her radar screen. Yet, because she doesn't do it regularly, when she does do it, she gets an employer's attention if the employer knows her. He or she will know that my wife is making a special effort to help a friend; people appreciate the extra efforts others make for friends. They usually give extra consideration to a letter from someone who's making an extra effort, particularly from a person who is not in the business world, who doesn't have a secretary or an office; e.g., a school teacher, a Sunday school teacher, a scout master, a camp counselor, a fellow meals-on-wheels worker. In other words, people who are good and caring people who don't have secretaries and office assistants to help them produce countless letters get special attention. And they deserve it. They're special people and their friends respect them. They can do a seemingly little thing that could make a big difference to a job seeker. A final comment on "little things." If a friend calls and asks for your help and you can't directly help—for whatever reason—at least try to help your friend think of things he or she has not done. Remind your friend of other friends who could help; tell your friend the name of a good recruiting agency; tell your friend about the hotline telephone numbers of employers; tell your friend about the latest article you have read on job searches; tell your friend stories of how other friends have gotten jobs. Even if you don't have contacts that could help a friend, help your friend with ideas and give him/her hope. Ideas are a powerful motivating force, and hope lifts the heart: "I'm stuck like a dope with a thing called hope, and I can't get it out of my

heart." (musical *South Pacific*)

CHAPTER 27
LEAVING PRIVATE-SECTOR JOBS

We've all heard, or at least heard of the song by Johnny Paycheck, "Take This Job and Shove It." I suspect we've all felt like saying it to our employer at one time or another. But feeling it and doing it are two very different things, and whether you do or don't do it could affect the rest of your life.

When I was fired from my Wall Street job, I concluded that I had to change professions. It was inconceivable to me that I could get a good reference from my ex-employer. Although I had been successful as a stockbroker at another stockbrokerage firm in Washington, D.C., I was convinced that that wouldn't make any difference. I had low productivity in my New York job and a negative attitude and nothing was going to change those facts. And because of that experience, I felt I had to start a new career in an entirely different field. I was thirty, my wife was pregnant, and we were broke. Changing careers wasn't easy; and it certainly wasn't fun.

A friend of mine's last year in a particular job was the most miserable of his professional career. Unlike me, however, it was also one of his most productive years in terms of client results and new business. It may seem unlikely for the two conditions to coexist, but they can.

My friend was miserable, so he did the smart thing. He improved his performance so he could leave on good terms. You should never leave an employer and tell him to "take this job and shove it." For the rest of your life, somebody, somewhere, will be asking you about a particular job and/or checking on your prior jobs. One negative reference could make the difference in your being chosen or not chosen for a new job or even for a promotion with an existing employer.

Having a good relationship with former employers is common sense. No one would really disagree unless leaving was necessary because of improper employer conduct such as sexual harassment or gender or racial discrimination. In those situations, most new employers would understand why you left and, indeed, may even consider your leaving under such circumstances necessary and courageous. But what about leaving because you just don't like the job or the people you work with? Maybe your bosses are a group of "preppies." Maybe you feel that they consider you lower-middle class and themselves upper class. Maybe they all went to prestigious schools and you only finished high school or attended a local college or community college and they keep reminding you of your educational insufficiencies in subtle ways. Maybe they are members of the country club, and your only club is the tennis and swim recreation center owned by your apartment or condo association. Maybe you're leaving simply because you cannot communicate with your bosses, or because the job is not interesting or challenging.

Whatever the reason for leaving a job, the reason is not nearly as important as *how* you leave. Leave on your best behavior; leave on your terms; leave when your production is the highest; leave when your employer is the happiest with your work product. Stated differently, if you intend to leave a job, you should give 110% for each remaining day you work before your departure. The more you dislike your job, and the more you want to leave, the harder you should work and the better should be your on-the-job attitude. Admittedly, this is not human nature, but it's a formula that works. Employers remember hard workers; they particularly remember hard workers with a good attitude. They tend to remember the good things about you if there are good things to remember.

Being remembered as a person with a strong work ethic and a good attitude should get you a good reference. But it could get you considerably more, namely, something we all need—an advocate. One advocate can do more for your career than many supporters. For example, a friend, who is one of my former bosses, recommended me to my present employer. Another friend, who is also a former boss, recommended me for political appointments, to other clients, and, in fact, gave me the highest possible recommendation: He employed me as a lawyer for his company after I left his employment.

Long ago, I learned a difficult lesson on Wall Street. I was unhappy and I let my employer know of my unhappiness. Somehow, I expected my employer to resolve my unhappiness. Isn't that ridiculous? What my employer corrected was having an unhappy person around him ("Pack that U-haul and go home, young man." "Do I have a choice?" "No, you don't.")

In short, a former employer can be your best employment contact. At a minimum, you should never alienate your former employers. More importantly, giving 110% and having a good attitude may well result in your having an advocate for life. "Doing the best at this moment puts you in the best place for the next moment." (Oprah Winfrey)

CHAPTER 28
LEAVING A GOVERNMENT JOB

A friend and I once pondered how we could get him out of his high-level state job into a private-sector job in an industry regulated by the government agency he worked for and yet remain credible with his former bosses. You see, there are restrictions on federal government employees leaving their jobs for the private sector and then lobbying their former employers and former fellow employees. At the state level, restrictions vary from agency to agency. People leaving government to work in industries that are subject to some form of oversight by the government agency they are leaving have to be careful of applicable conflict-of-interest rules. They also have to be careful not to offend their former government agency leader.

Now, back to my friend who once held a high-level state government job. He was offered the chief financial officer's (CFO's) job for a $300-million-a-year company regulated by the state agency where he was employed. Because the company that offered him the job was regulated by the agency, and past employees who "jumped ship" for regulated companies became *persona non grata* at the regulatory agency, my friend was concerned that if he left his government job to take the new position with the regulated company, he would be "burning his bridges," something he absolutely could not do. His principal responsibility with his new employer would be making financial filings with, and testifying before, the agency he was leaving. He certainly couldn't afford to leave and alienate the state agency's head. He also couldn't afford not to leave. The financial and career opportunity differences in the two jobs were significant.

I'll tell you the end of the story later in this section, but first, you may like to hear about our plan to get him out of state government and into the regulated company without alienating the state agency's head. We decided to ask a particular "Big 8" accounting firm to hire my friend. Inasmuch as he was a C.P.A. and had considerable accounting experience, it was plausible that he would be recruited by a major accounting firm. It also seemed to us that if an accounting firm hired him, and if he left the accounting firm in a few months or a year for the regulated company, he would not be viewed as "jumping ship" from the regulatory agency to a regulated company. I also believed that the then "Big 8" accounting firm would welcome the opportunity to assist my friend just for the opportunity to know him better when he was in his new job. Simply put, I wanted the accounting firm to "launder" my friend so he would not be considered a government employee that jumped ship to work for a regulated company. To my pleasant surprise, the accounting firm agreed. True, the deal wasn't in writing and no one would acknowledge our plan today, but it was a creative idea. It was the only way we felt we could guarantee my friend employment in his new position without running the risk of alienating his former agency heads. We did not believe that they would be concerned a year later. After all, he was an exceptionally qualified employee; the fact that another opportunity came along a year later would not surprise anyone.

Today, my friend is the CFO with the regulated company and he enjoys the highest possible credibility with his former state agency. Furthermore, he made the change without the necessity of anyone's "laundering" him on the payroll. He took the direct approach and told the state agency heads the reason for his decision to leave. They understood perfectly that it was a major career opportunity and, in fact, a once-in-a-lifetime opportunity. They encouraged him to take the new position and gave him their blessings.

We still talk about our plan to "launder" him through a "Big 8" accounting firm and how we believe it would have worked. We chuckle about our "laundering" scheme. But we both remember the best lesson of all; always be honest with your employer and *never, never* burn bridges behind you when you leave government. The most important asset any of us has in the business world is our integrity. Schemes may work in the short run, but in the long run schemers get schemed. "Goodness is the only investment that never fails." (Henry David Thoreau) As lawyers say about other lawyers who overreach in particular cases, "What goes around comes around." The last thing a government employee can afford to do is to move to a private-sector job that deals with the agency he left, and then have his prior bad relationship "come around." Every business needs government at one time or another. If a particular agency's employees don't like you, an employer who deals with that agency won't have anything to do with you. And no one can blame him or her. Actions of government agencies often can mean everything to businesses.

Leaving government? Leave on the right foot. "People who bite the hand that feeds them usually lick the boot that kicks them." (Eric Hoffer)

CHAPTER 29
WHAT GOES AROUND COMES AROUND

When we are unpleasant to others in either our professional or personal lives, eventually our unpleasantness comes back around to haunt us. And it's no fun being on the receiving end of unpleasant statements or criticisms. No fun at all. Fortunately, the opposite is true. When we are pleasant to others, eventually our pleasantness comes back around to us. That is fun.

When we're helpful to friends, our help comes back around in the form of help from our friends. For example, the friend in the last chapter that I tried to help locate a job with a "Big 8" accounting firm is the special person in chapter 5 who helped me find employment for the daughter of a good friend and the daughter of a good client. In fact, he hired both as a favor to me (and he never regretted it). It is remarkable how my small gesture to help him generated boundless goodwill from him toward me. This is the unexpected joy of helping others; they will help you and your friends, and they will do it willingly and enthusiastically. "He who sows sparingly will also reap sparingly, and he who sows bountifully will also reap bountifully." (2 Corinthians 9, 6)

I helped a friend find a job and, without any prompting on my part, he recommended me for a job in 1980 to a friend of his at Georgia Power Company who, because of his friendship with my friend, recommended me to Duke Power Company. How did the individual at Georgia Power know enough about me to recommend me to Duke Power? He didn't. He was relying on his friend's confidence in me. Friends trust each other; he trusted his friend.

Help others and you don't have to worry about getting help. "The only things we ever keep are what we give away." (Louis Ginsberg)

CHAPTER 30

A TRUE FRIEND

For most of us, a true friend is a one-of-a-kind friend. It is the person we trust the most; the person we share our innermost secrets with; the person about whom we never have to worry whether he or she will help us; our lifelong childhood friend; our spouses; a parent or a sibling. Most of us group our friends into various categories. We have work friends, high-school friends, college friends, church friends, and other such friends. They are friends but, to be sure, they're not all "true" friends.

In writing this book and recollecting the people I've tried to help with jobs over the years, I consider virtually everyone a friend. Even if they weren't when we started working together, we soon became friends. Yet, they're clearly not a friend such as my wife, or a neighbor I've known for thirty years whose children have grown up with my children, or a colleague I've worked with for twenty years. They're clearly not a friend such as the sergeant who helped me survive in the military; or the friend who was always there for me in an emergency.

What I've come to realize in this cathartic process is the obvious. There are friends and there are friends. My wife is a friend but a very different type of friend from my military friend. My fellow workers are very different types of friends from childhood friends; clients are often friends you never see again after you work with them but, nevertheless, they were friends for a while. High school teachers, Sunday school teachers, boy scout and girl scout buddies are friends but, again, very different types of friends from others. Yet, they are all still friends.

This self-analysis leads me to a different conclusion about friends as I conclude this book compared to when I started it. I started with a relatively narrow view of a friend. Mine was similar to Aristotle's definition: "Friendship is a single soul dwelling in two bodies." Yet, with all due respect to Aristotle, few of us have a friend who is our twin soulmate. We have different friends at different times and places in our lives, and we have a different relationship with each friend.

What is important is not so much to have the perfect friend, a "true" friend. What is important in a friend is probably best stated by Sidney Smith, an English clergyman and writer and master of wit and satire, in the early 1800s: "Life is to be fortified by many friendships. To love, and to be loved, is the greatest happiness of existence." But, of course, to have friends you have to be a friend. To quote another accomplished and talented Englishman writer, William Shakespeare, "They do not love that do now show their love."

CONCLUSION

Learning of a good job opportunity is hard; getting an interview for the job is even harder; and getting the particular job could be harder than solving the "Rubik's Cube." In other words, getting a good job is hard as hell for most of us.

But where there is a will, there is a way. Start with a plan, call on your friends, find an advocate, and "gut it out." It will all come together sooner or later. In fact, when it happens it will probably be the result of something totally unexpected and you will immediately think that finding the right job was luck. But it won't be luck. It will be because of persistence; it will be because of something a friend did or said; it will be because you're qualified; it will be because of inextricably linked circumstances that you won't be able to explain. But it won't be mere luck.

Along the way, you may shoot a silver bullet or two (or a friend will); you may contact a politician (or a friend will); you may make a cold call or two (because you didn't have anything else to do that day); and you might read the want ads (in the doctor's office, of course). You may even "beef up" your résumé from time to time (knowing that you're wasting time, but you'll do it anyway).

You will eventually find your job. And when all is said and done and you look back over your career and "smell the roses," you won't remember all the telephone calls, letters, applications, and interviews. You won't even remember many of the people you worked with. You will, however, remember your mentors. They're the friends who pulled you up and pushed you up; they made you succeed in spite of yourself. To paraphrase the Hallmark card slogan, they cared enough to do their very best for you, and it ultimately paid off for you. You, in turn, will repay them by caring enough to do your very best for others. You will be the friend, the advocate, the mentor. And you will be forever glad you were. As Ralph Waldo Emerson said, "It is one of the most beautiful compensations of this life that no man can sincerely try to help another without helping himself."

CPSIA information can be obtained
at www.ICGtesting.com
Printed in the USA
BVHW041109040423
661730BV00001B/5